HARLEY-DAVIDSON

A PICTORIAL CELEBRATION

HARLEY-DAVIDSON

A PICTORIAL CELEBRATION

MALCOLM BIRKITT

OSPREY
AUTOMOTIVE

First published in 1993 by Osprey Publishing, an imprint
of Reed Consumer Books Limited, Michelin House,
81 Fulham Road, London SW3 6RB

Cataloguing in Publication Data for this title is available
from the British Library

ISBN 1 85532 241 2

Editor Shaun Barrington
Page design Paul Kime
Printed in Italy

CONTENTS

CHAPTER ONE

IN THE BEGINNING...

Come the year 2003 Harley-Davidson – America's legendary motorcycle manufacturer – should be celebrating a remarkable centenary. The company has grown from the humblest origins, and somehow survived all kinds of fluctuating fortunes along the way to their present pre-eminence. Arthur Davidson and William S Harley, who initially met in 1901, first began tinkering with two-wheelers in a tiny Milwaukee shed just 15 feet by 10 feet, helped out by two of Davidson's brothers. Bill was the guy with pencil, while Art wielded the spanners. But the first machines hardly breathed fire – the small displacement four-stroke single cylinder engine of the first "Silent Grey Fellow" pushed out a very modest 3 horsepower and was equipped with belt-driven rear wheel.

Arthur's brother, Walter Davidson, played a significant role by introducing to the fledgling company a German engineer with experience in motorcycle production. The first three bikes constructed were virtually hand-made, but demand soon exceeded supply and the company had to take on more workers, producing 50 motorcycles in the year 1906. Despite the fact that both founders of the company were skilled mechanics, they soon came to the conclusion

that they could not cope with mass production; the result was that Bill Harley enrolled in a four-year course at the University of Wisconsin. He later became the technical manager of the company while the Davidson brothers took care of the production and sales. By 1907, H-D Inc had been formed and production had shifted to the present Juneau Avenue address. Two years later, the first Harley with a V-twin engine was made. It had cylinders splayed at a 45° angle, like the modern bikes, but churned out a paltry 7 bhp – not too much rumble there. Less than a decade later, Harleys were ridden by the public, police, competition riders and most importantly, the military. During the First World War, some 20,000 machines saw active service, and enabled the first US soldiers to press into Germany in 1918.

With the war out of the way, Harley-Davidson entered the 1920s like the rest of America – in a mood of optimism. Production expanded, new models were introduced with improved engines and features, and bike sales took off. A host of V-twins contributed plenty of noise to the "Roaring Twenties". Around this time a Harley even won the first ever moto-cross, at Camberley, Surrey, England.

LEFT *The insinuation that real touring bikes only started to appear in America in 1975, with the first Honda Gold Wing, is a notion that's highly offensive to Harley-Davidson enthusiasts. Harleys have criss-crossed the States since the '30s and the FLH "King of the Highway" had been around since 1957! The legendary Electra-Glide first hit the highways in 1965, and is still going strong, of course; albeit in larger and more powerful 1340 cc form.*

ABOVE *In 1969, Honda stunned America with the launch of the advanced, ohc four-cylinder, disc-braked CB750. Over in Milwaukee, the Electra Glide of the same era illustrates that Harley-Davidson was rather stuck in a technological time-warp. Curiously there were many who preferred their '70s bikes to act like '50s machinery, hence the big drum brakes, tank-mounted instruments and sprung single seat. Discs finally appeared on the FLH tourers in '72. Except for upping the engine's capacity cubes to 1340 cc, the Electra Glide has remained surprisingly unchanged since then. Proof, many would say, of the correctness of the original concept.*

ABOVE *What greater pleasure is there than taking a big-bore V-twin out for an evening blast? This immaculate Shovelhead FLH looks in better condition than when it left the factory twenty-five years ago! Boulevard cruising, often two up as here, is what makes many enthusiasts keep coming back to a Harley year after year.*

RIGHT *After more than eighty years of competition success, Harley-Davidsons still create more than their share of interest on tarmac circuits and dirt tracks on both sides of the Atlantic. Currently 883 cc Sportster racing is both affordable and very competitive, thanks to the near-production specifications of everyone's machines. Brit racer Nigel Gale campaigned his bike at Daytona in 1991 and scraped home in front by the narrowest of margins. The 883 Sportster racing formula has now spread across the Atlantic and 1992 has seen a national series at most of the British short circuit venues.* (David Goldman)

CHAPTER TWO

IRON ICON

More than any other bike manufacturer, Harley-Davidson understands that a riders' relationship with his motorcycle takes place, if you'll pardon the expression, mainly between the ears, not between the legs. H-D Inc isn't attempting to create the fastest or best handling two-wheel projectiles on the road, but bikes which project an image, an idea, a look, and represent a piece of pure Americana. Forget that a Harley is slow and vibrates enough to blur your vision and loosen those fillings, because we're talking about dreams. The aura surrounding the humble metal now extends beyond mere motorcycling. Advertisers seeking a future-retro association for their products jostle to be the next to use the bike's raking profile gliding across the screen, even though they're trying to sell you jeans or an aftershave.

On the broader scale, a Harley represents a symbol of America as much as the Stars and Stripes, the Empire State or the Statue of Liberty. The decision to purchase one of the USA's sole surviving motorcycle makers' machines can be interpreted as an act of unbridled patriotism. On a more personal, individual level, a Harley-Davidson retains a tangible human quality and scale, despite its considerable dimensions. Owning one brings membership of a cult, and a gateway to another lifestyle that picks you out from the crowd. Aboard your Harley you flout conformism. The company deserves full marks for expertly milking every drop of appeal their throwback designs generate.

The big V-twins are obviously designed and built by real people, people who clearly ride bikes and enjoy them. In comparison, virtually all imported machines carry the unmistakable whiff of computer programs, wind tunnels and robotised mass-production. In other words, they're appliances which work perfectly and function with extraordinary efficiency. In a word, boring.

Efficiency is not a word you'd immediately think of with regard to the imperfect Harley. These endearingly "conservative" bikes operate within a relatively confined performance envelope, cough when cold, vibrate like a concrete mixer in various speed bands, have moderate cornering ability and take an era to stop. But it is these very flaws that endears the rider to his machine, that creates a relationship between man and metal. You don't take it for granted, you get to know its weaknesses, how to treat it, and nurse it along. Reciprocally, if you're feeling

low, the bike puts the smile back on your face.

There's an unarguable massiveness about a stationary Harley, a bold mechanical quality and timelessness in sharp contrast to the seamless efficiency and modernity of Japanese machines. Further differences are apparent on the move – a Harley has a locomotive-like feel and look, and riders are made very much aware of the powerful forces of internal combustion. Imported bikes, regardless of how they ape the Harley V-twin, cannot match it for visceral feel. They lack the emotional content that is part and parcel of every Harley, replacing it with calculated efficiency and ultimate performance. This aspect of the Harley, its nostalgic – but fully market aware – embrace of tradition is what attracts many riders, yet repels others. There's little sitting on the fence on the subject of Harley-Davidson – you either love them or loathe them.

For many the Harley-Davidson motorcycle neatly encapsulates the notion of freedom, nostalgia and individualism they seek in their crowded, hurried lives. Just having one in the garage imbues the owner

Harley-Davidsons are glory machines to be seen on. The bike lends to its owner an aura of rebellion, freedom and style that no other marque can conjure. The first semblance of this curious phenomenon was nurtured in the '50s, when Marlon Brando looked mean and moody on a bike in the film The Wild One. *The mere fact that it wasn't a Harley he straddled has been submerged as the Milwaukee myth has multiplied. Some people even think Steve McQueen leapt barbed-wire fencing on one! And further fuel was poured on the flames in the late '60s with* Naked under Leather *(British title* Girl on a Motorcycle) *starring Marianne Faithfull, closely followed by the cult US movie* Easy Rider. *After that, a Harley-Davidson became de rigeur for any celebrity seeking to evoke that defiant posture. Even a youthful, pouting Brigitte Bardot got in on the act in a song written for her by Serge Gainsbourg. "I've no need of anyone, on my Harley-Davidson, I recognise no-one, on my Harley-Davidson" she drooled. Despite the fact that the sex kitten turned animal lover never threw a leg over a hog, those lyrics still have an uncannily powerful resonance even today.*

with a liberated feeling, like having your own steed tied up on a rail and ready to go. Whether a rider covers five or fifty-five thousand miles a year on two wheels, that feeling remains the same. Though these cowboy-like associations seem rather far fetched as we segue into the 21st century, they represent a dream. The American dream of freedom.

LEFT *There are more eagles down on Main Street than ever congregate in the wild. This and other symbols of American iconography such as the Stars and Stripes are frequently interwoven with the H-D logo in custom paintwork. Tank artwork has become increasingly popular over the years; attend any Harley-Davidson gathering and you can't fail to be impressed by the sheer creative brilliance of the striking paint jobs.*

ABOVE *Americans are the most patriotic people you'll ever meet, anywhere on this often crazy planet. Fiercely proud of their country, they fly the flag at the drop of a hat. In the Seventies, Harley even offered a fender-mounted flag pole as a factory-approved accessory. Ask yourself this question if you don't believe all this nationalistic hokum. How many stars of stage and screen, seeking to reinforce their allegiance to the all-American dream, do you see riding around on bikes that roll out of Hammamatsu? Exactly.*

DYNA GLIDE

The Stars & Stripes provide a fitting backdrop to a 1991 Sturgis, finished in purposeful black, naturally. While black normally represents an absence of light – a negative thing – Harley black is far more positive, as it announces the presence of mass. The FXDB was the first of a new wave of machines with a Dyna Glide chassis, which further emphasised the low-slung lines. Long 33.1 inch forks with a 32° rake, long chaincase engine and 1 inch longer swinging arm all add up to the L-O-N-G look. Wheelbase was 65.5 inches and dry weight a tad under 600lbs. Clearly visible are the risers that lift the handlebars 4 inches up and about 2.5 inches back. In going after the look, Harley sometimes find form overrides function, as anyone who has thrown a leg over the Sturgis will have discovered. While the worst of the vibes are pleasantly subdued, especially at cruising speeds, the long low look compromises suspension operation. The front fork, because of its steep rake, gives a somewhat harsh ride, and the rear wheel is given only 3 inches of travel. On poor surfaces you feel every ripple, while serious ridges can bump the seat upwards and throw the rider vertically. Only 1700 of the all black limited edition were produced. The next Dyna Glide to arrive was the dual disc braked FXDB Daytona, another limited edition of 1700. Its gold cast wheels rolled out to commemorate the 50th anniversary of Daytona Raceweek. Also new for 1992 was the first mass produced Dyna Glide, the FXDC Dyna Glide Custom, silver, black, aluminium and, um, oh yes, chrome. *(Mac McDiarmid)*

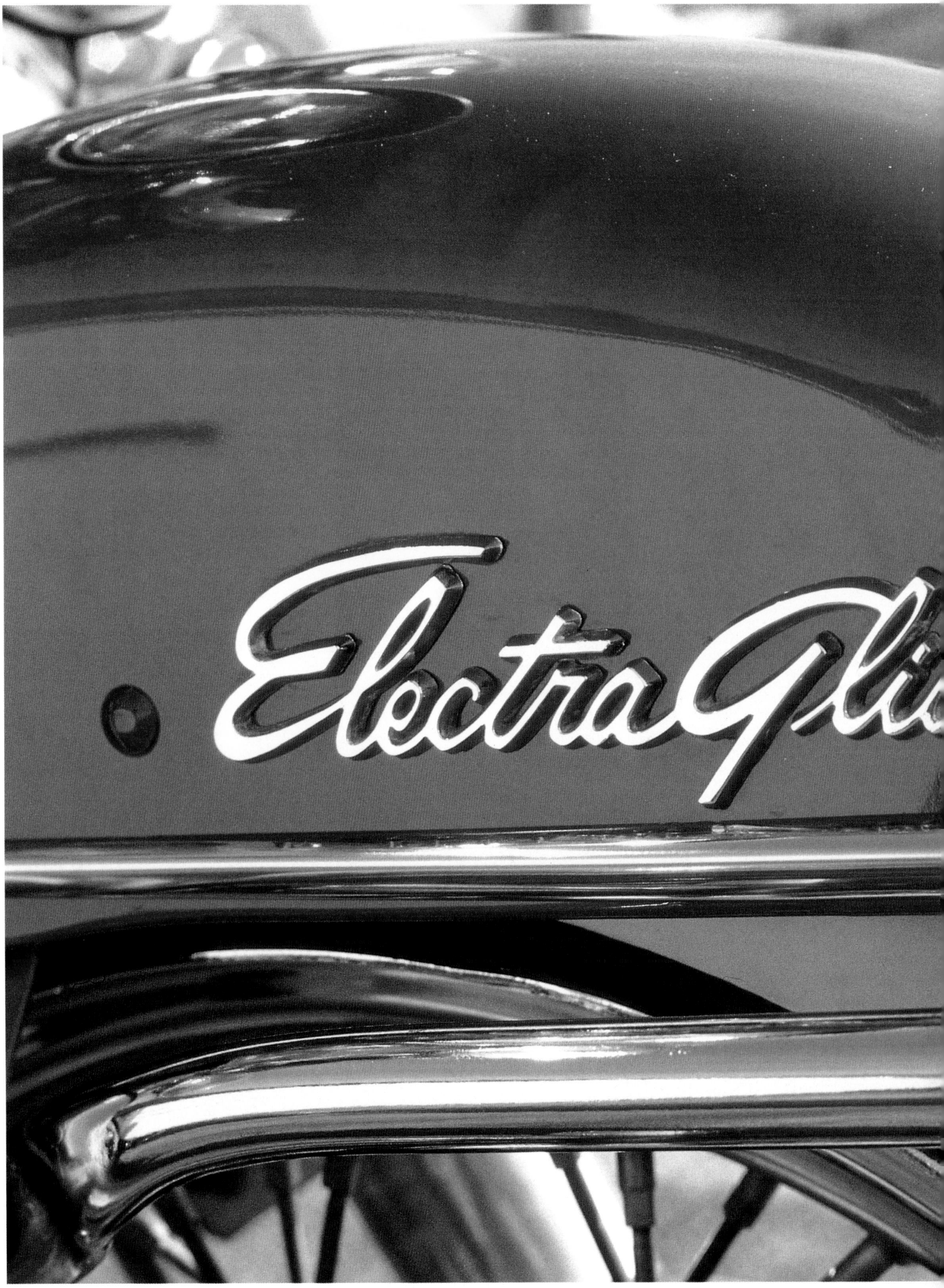
Electra

Why describe Harley's big tourer as an FLH, when "Electra Glide" is the best label ever handed out to any two-wheeler? This metal badge has the power to make grown men turn weak at the knees. Names mean more to people than mere numbers, something the mighty Japanese marketing machine seems unable to comprehend. Europeans and Harley Davidson do, hence Electra Glide, Super Glide Sportster et al.

PREVIOUS PAGES *Just as cowboys once tethered their weary horses outside the saloon, a couple of weary, not to mention thirsty, journalists crossing the States rest their iron steeds after another long day in the saddle. The Old Dodge City weatherboarding goes well with the nostalgic image that all Harleys impart. (Mac McDiarmid)*

ABOVE *Harley-Davidson's Electra Glide is the quintessential American motorcycle. That characteristic, daringly curvaceous half-painted fairing first appeared in 1969, as an alternative to the flat police-type plain screen. Perhaps it was something to do with the fact that Milwaukee had acquired a fibreglass plant about this time that made Harley fit them on a FLH. Whatever the*

reason, the same fairing is still with us on the present Electra Glide. Protection for the rider and passenger is excellent, as the air is calm behind the screen, and dry even in a downpour. The screen height is also adjustable. On top of all these good functions, it still looks terrific.

RIGHT *As American as the Empire State, Stars and Stripes, or Uncle Sam himself – that's the automatic association that the name Harley-Davidson conjures up. Pointing out that suspension, carburettor and other bits emanate from the land of the rising sun isn't being frank, though – it's an act akin to heresy. Don't mention these trifling details to any Harley fan if you prefer your features the way they're currently arranged.*

ABOVE *The link between competition success and shifting road bikes off the showroom floor is a hard one to prove. But there's surely something in it, even though most riders don't press their pavement Harleys very hard. For real speed and extreme angles of lean, it's best to park up the road bike and watch the 883 cc Sportster racers let it all hang out. Formula allows for several changes including engine tuning, exhaust and suspension, but basics including engine casing, frame and petrol tank must remain the same.*

RIGHT *FXRS Low Rider, doing what it does best, cruising. The revamp for 1988 would include a built-in fuel gauge for the twin-cap gas tank, and new 39 mm fork to replace the earlier 35 mm unit, the latter a change across the board for all FXR and XL models.*

CHAPTER THREE

VENERABLE V-TWIN

Though the eagle first flew in 1903, it was not until six years later that a V-twin – the engine configuration with which the Harley-Davidson marque is indelibly associated – was first used in a motorcycle. This William Harley-designed mill adopted the familiar 45° angle between the pots – a completely arbitrary decision, apparently. This machine was propelled up to 60mph by its far from rumbling 7bhp 61 cu in (999 cc) motor – nevertheless a healthy portent of the large displacement motors to come.

1921 saw the debut of the enduring 74 cu in (1212 cc) V-twin, an engine size which featured in the range for almost sixty years. Of almost equal production longevity was the 45 cu in side-valve V-twin (737 cc), which first appeared in 1929. these rugged, reliable units were made in vast numbers for war use, and powered motorcycles until 1952. Production of the 45 continued right through until 1974 – it was fitted into the Servi-Car. This inexpensive three-wheeler used for police and an assortment of delivery purposes was Harley's response to a calamitous decline in the bike industry caused by the Depression.

In 1936 the legendary ohv "Knucklehead" V-twin saw the light of day. Why the company chose to launch such an important new model in 1936 has always been one of the great Harley-Davidson mysteries and remains unanswered, at least officially, to this day. Motorcycle sales in the early and mid 1930s were poor to say the least, motorcycle enthusiasm in the States was at an all-time low (only about 100,000 machines were registered across the USA at the time), whilst the only surviving specialist magazine had been reduced to a few hundred loyal readers.

But maybe it was seen as the last throw of the dice, in the hope that it would turn the tide. In fact, the Knucklehead became one of Harley-Davidson's greatest ever success stories. Officially coded G/E, the motor featured ohv (overhead valve) intake and exhaust with both valves in the head. This wasn't a fresh idea: Harley-Davidson and rivals Indian (and several other marques) had done it before, notably with competition bikes: some going as far as four valves per cylinder and even the luxury of overhead camshafts on their racers as far back as the teens. But such systems were generally considered noisy and more expensive to produce and maintain. So side valves, "flatheads" in the slang of the day, had ruled supreme on American-made roadsters, both bikes and

cars. Therefore the Milwaukee company could be seen to have gambled heavily by breaking with tradition in a time of recession.

Engine capacity was 61 cu in initially, enlarged to 74 cu in in 1942. Cast iron cylinders were featured, with the characteristic heads of the same material. This was the first Harley fitted with a dry sump lubrication system, whereby oil is returned to a holding tank after doing its stuff around the engine. Unfortunately plenty of it leaked out of the motor too, due to an unresolved crankcase vacuum and poor seals, joints and mating surfaces.

To rectify these problems, a new engine complete with hydraulic valve lifters was launched in 1948 – the "Panhead". Cast iron barrels were now topped with aluminium alloy heads shaped like baking pans (baking tins to British readers!), and a revised lubrication system was employed. Redesigned internal oilways largely cured the oil consumption and leak problems, though the felt pads glued to the inside of the covers to recirculate oil sometimes worked loose. This design was available in two

Plentiful WL and WLA 45 cu in/737 cc side-valve models were produced from 1929 onwards, but they're now collector's pieces. Harley had an ohv engine earlier, but switched to side-valve to compete with the Indian engine of the same configuration that was beating the Harley in competition. The side-valve, with fewer parts, was also cheaper and easier to manufacture – and maintain.

engine sizes – 61 cu in and 74 cu in – and went on to power the first Electra Glide model in 1965.

Because of the Panhead's reputation for chewing up chains and the odd main bearing failure, Harley-Davidson brought out a "new" engine in 1966 – new meaning a fresh top-end on a proven bottom end. So the "Shovelhead" – so-called because its rocker cover resembled coal shovels in someone's fevered imagination – was in reality a "Panhead" with redesigned cylinders and heads. External oil lines were also in evidence once again. Originally the engine featured a generator, but in 1976 a modified design with a crankshaft-mounted alternator was

introduced. Two years later engine displacement was upped to 80 cu in (1340 cc) and electronic ignition was fitted. Sadly oil leaks still dogged the Shovelhead.

Eighteen years on in 1984, Harley finally solved the oil loss problems when they introduced the "Blockhead" motor or V-2 Evolution motor – the latter name stuck because it was clearly descended from the 1936 61E Knucklehead, while Blockhead didn't quite carry the right message. The new mill made 10% more power and 15% more torque, but tipped the scales some 20lbs lighter. Aluminium heads and barrels with iron liners dissipated heat evenly and efficiently, while the 80 cu in mill also showed modest oil consumption and excellent reliability.

In many ways, the unfolding story of the mighty V-twin typifies Harley-Davidson's unspoken philosophy. There's just one basic rule involved – if it works, don't change it. After three-quarters of a century, however, the aptly titled Evolution design confirmed that the V-twin had finally come of age.

ABOVE *So that's what goes on inside a 1200 Sportster! Straightforward engineering means that most routine servicing can still be handled by the owner. Harley-Davidson have remained faithful to the V-twin configuration for over eighty years, because it's a durable engine that can be rebuilt many times over. The Evolution motor launched in 1984 has proved a tough and reliable unit, capable of pumping out double the stock horsepower without ripping itself apart. Tales of motors approaching 200,000 miles without major surgery are not uncommon – when stripped there was a little wear, naturally, but the engines remained strong.*

RIGHT *Sensuous curves of XR750 Sportster-lookalike exhaust pipes scream muscular power. That Milwaukee music is created by the front piston first and then, 315° of crankshaft rotation later, the rear one. That leaves an interval of 405° before the front fires again, leading to that wonderful ba-bump, ba-bump lop-sided beat.*

LEFT *Harley V-twins have always had bags of torque, but the flexibility of the 1340 cc Evolution motor is outstanding. This V-twin will lope along in fifth gear at low speeds without bogging down. When set up properly, a modern Harley will start easily, warm up quickly and rarely give a cough, thanks to the new 40mm (Japanese!) Keihin constant-velocity carburettor. Altered cam profiles, with more lift and duration, also brought subtle improvements to driveability in 1990. The redline is at just 5200rpm, at which time the Harley is churning out a modest 72 bhp. More pertinent is the flat torque curve, which means that useful power is available anywhere in the rev range. For the record, peak torque occurs at 4000rpm. Hydraulic tappets, first seen back in 1948, mean top end maintenance is minimal – overhauls every 50,000 miles are recommended.*

ABOVE *A major plus of the along-the-frame V-twin engine layout is that it gives a slim profile when viewed from the front. But some of the advantage is lost as the air cleaner cover protrudes considerably, and the riders right leg has to bend around it. This tank and seat off view reveals the sturdy braced frame with its duplex rails to cradle the massive motor, which is rigidly mounted in Softail models. Concealed rear suspension also helps the engine to dominate the appearance.*

SO WHAT'S NEW?

Launched in 1965, the first FLH Electra Glide featured the elderly 74 cu in/1212 cc Panhead V-twin (below). This was soon replaced by the Shovelhead engine for the 1966 model year – a design that saw service for eighteen years. Both motors employed the familiar gear-driven camshaft down in the crankcase, operating the valves via pushrods and rockers. Cam followers were hydraulic, which automatically adjusted to the correct valve clearances. A four-speed transmission was also employed by both mills, the five-speed only coming into production in the latter years of the Shovelhead's life. Unlike the Sportster's mill, that of the Electra Glide is truly antique in appearance. As both exhausts are routed to the offside, the nearside of 1340 cc Evolution motor (right) is somewhat plain. Until, that is, a series of gold-plated accessories are fitted. Those heel and toe gear levers can be a squeeze for riders with large feet. Engines in Softail models use the long primary chaincase, which gives an extra inch between the crankshaft and clutch centres compared to FXR bikes. That may not sound much, but any additional length all contributes to the deliberate long, low profile.

ABOVE LEFT *The Shovelhead motor misfired, rattled and vibrated its way through the best part of two decades. Even shortish trips distressed the motor sufficiently to shake off domed nuts or fracture brackets. Longer runs resulted in bikes returning weighing considerably less than when they had set off, as an assortment of small items had been distributed along the road at regular intervals. 1984-on Evolution machines are almost boring in comparison, as after any kind of trip the motorcycle comprises the same number of parts as when it set off!*

LEFT *Locomotive-like power of mammoth 80 cu in/1340 cc V-twin first hit the road in 1978 in Shovelhead guise. It had larger pistons – up to 88.8mm – and a longer stroke – now 108mm – over the 74 cu in/1212 cc unit. It even boasted electronic ignition for the first time. The 80-incher makes a noise like a train, with plenty of mechanical accompaniment, but unlike the Jap multis, the biggest Harley powerplant never feels frenzied. If vibration is damped it operates with a pleasing, controlled thunder below 3000 rpm. It's still a willing unit above that figure, but starts to feel less happy.*

ABOVE *If you thought Harley just bolted the 80 inch V-twin straight into the frame, you'd be wrong. Bikes in the Softail range mount the engine so that a vertical line bisects the V of the cylinders. FXR-type machines such as this angle the engine forward a touch – the same bisecting line is now 2° out of plumb. On bikes using the Dyna chassis, such as the Sturgis, the engine is tilted 4° back, permitting the engine and transmission to be mounted further forward. This alters weight distribution subtly towards the front wheel, enhancing high-speed stability. Machine is a Sport Glide. It now comes with belt drive and dual front discs as standard.*

LEFT *Why was the V-twin layout adopted? Because it gave a wide power band and excellent low-end torque in a durable, compact and easy to maintain package. There was only one carburettor needed to supply fuel to both cylinders, and fewer parts than a multi-cylinder engine. The along-the frame V-twin permits the largest capacity in the narrowest width, can be placed low in the frame for a low centre of gravity and seat height. This improves stability and enables a machine to be more easily manoeuvred at low speeds and at standstill. Also no other engine emits such a noise – there's something undeniably satisfying about the distinctive rumble of the Harley V-twin. You can virtually see that heavy flywheel and those monstrous pistons working.*

ABOVE *Everybody who's ridden an 80-incher knows that Harley produce the definitive cruising motorcycle powerplant. Power is available in bucketfuls, at any rpm you care to mention. From idle to redline, the torque curve never dips below 55 pounds-feet, and the peak of the curve, if that is the right term, is 62 pound-feet at 3000 rpm – more than many large displacement multis. The cold figures translate into massive reserves of power out on the tarmac. Try trundling down to 25 mph in top, for instance, then whacking open the throttle. The great shuddering V-twin erupts into life, and within the blink of an eye your speed has tripled, accompanied by a glorious booming racket. There's simply no other experience like it. Custom Softail shown is hard evidence that nostalgia sells motorcycles, at least for Harley-Davidson.*

Nearly thirty years after the electric start first appeared on a Harley-Davidson motorcycle, coaxing the two giant pistons into life still has that agricultural aura. Whereas a sanitised Jap bike starts quietly and efficiently, pressing the button on a modern Harley is still an experience. First there's a loud thunk as the starter pinion goes in, a great pregnant wheeze for a few seconds, some heavy-duty spinning until the lump catches, followed by an assortment of bangs and pops while the reluctant cold metal rubs the sleep from its eyes. Firing up an already hot motor is easier, but only just. That's not the end of the drama. Apply pressure to the gear lever to select first and there's a loud c-r-runch, accompanied by the rattle of the double-row primary chain inside the cover. Let the clutch out slowly while twisting the throttle a tad, ignore the thrashing noises, and the plot hardly seems to change revs but speed is piled on very rapidly. Watchers can hear the low chuf-chuf of the flat exhaust note, but all the rider is aware of is the feeling of massive, stomping flywheel power. Terrific! Top speed is well in excess of 100mph, but three things prevent anyone riding at such velocities. These are speed limits, wind pressure on unfaired machines and the fact that at anything over 80mph, the 80 cu in/1340 cc V-twin loses its equilibrium. As the motor nears 5000rpm – the kind of revs that oriental machines are just approaching the powerband – the Harley feels increasingly harassed.

ABOVE *1984 saw Harley-Davidson take yet another step forward to make its bikes fitting for the age – the Evolution engine appeared to replace the old "fry-your-legs" Shovelhead design. With its new heads, barrels and pistons, it was hailed by Harley as smoother, more powerful and efficient yet cooler running. This was the result of various improvements in areas such as combustion chamber design, breathing, valve timing and ignition. Put them all together and the Evolution V-twin gives a longer life, less noise and easier maintenance. Best of all, oil consumption is negligible – when the Shovelhead wasn't drinking the glurpy stuff at an alarming rate it leaked from numerous "mated" surfaces. The Evolution-powered bikes can be ridden for days without worrying about the mark on the dipstick. Sportsters also received the Evolution mill from 1986.*

ABOVE RIGHT *Whereas Japanese factory customs with their electric motor characteristics manage to reduce any amount of power and torque to a level of blandness only exceeded by processed cheese, no rider can miss the primordial character of the lazy V-twin that powers every Harley-Davidson. The absence of high-tech ensures that you can make sense of what's happening between the throttle and rear tyre. This "open-air" Electric Glide is minus usual fairing to give its rider an old style feel.*

RIGHT *The way it lopes unhurriedly along is the best attribute of the 80 cu in/1340 cc Harley engine. At 60mph, it spins at just 2800rpm – you can almost recognise which cylinder each bang comes from. The big-bore pushrod V-twin isn't just an engine – it's a national monument. Lucky man who owns this superb Electra Glide Classic model, the envy of many. Although top speed is only around 100 mph, its street cred and touring ability are legendary.*

LEFT *Post-'84 Evolution motor doesn't look that different to its Shovelhead daddy, but represents a quantum leap forward. Five years on the drawing board and $15 million of development has catapulted the Harley V-twin into the present, but not at the expense of losing the earlier character. The basic design remains as overhead valve and two valves per cylinder, but a 15% increase in torque is available via improved cam timing and design. Harley-Davidson chose not to alter the other curious aspect of their V-twin – the fact that the rear cylinder is directly behind the front one, and not offset. This would provide better cooling for the rear pot, and allow the conrods to ride side by side on the crankshaft. Instead Harleys use a fork arrangement, with the front rod inside the other. Some owners opt for a cooler heat range spark plug in the rear cylinder, especially if any speed work is to be undertaken.*

ABOVE *For anyone who speaks Harley's language – that's torque with a capital T – Sportster engines piled up to the ceiling make a mouthwatering sight. The unit construction V-twin is available in two sizes – regular 883 cc and a serious 1200 cc. Just imagine how much value is contained on this racking!* (Mac McDiarmid)

OVERLEAF *Gradients don't faze the 80 cubic inches that powers the Electra Glide Classic. Rarely is a downchange from top gear needed, such is the torque of the big V-twin. Ride quality and the general plushness of the seat and suspension ensure vast distances can be covered in a single day; a vital requirement in the USA, if not in Europe!* (Mac McDiarmid)

CHAPTER FOUR

HOME ON THE RANGE

In a bid to recapture the hearts of those countless motorcyclists disenchanted with a surfeit of fibreglass-enveloped high-tech, most manufacturers have recently looped back and resorted to production of classic-styled retro-bikes. Harley-Davidson, on the other hand, just keep building the same old machines, albeit within a framework of constant refinement. Thumb through the glossy catalogues of Milwaukee's finest and you can't miss how period styling hangs together with modern function. Marque logos on teardrop tanks or springer forks sit comfortably with electronic ignition and disc brakes.

In the hard-bitten world of the 1990s Harley-Davidson survives, thrives even, because it has a product which is unique, and people seeking identity will pay for something that's distinctive. Though other materials offer lighter weight or greater strength, bikes wearing a Harley badge continue to be crafted from real steel, and contain that sturdy feel which Americans still associate with quality. Harleys can't, or simply won't, compete with the ultimate performance available via Japanese machinery. Instead, they carve a niche in the motorcycle market which is entirely their own.

Though unabashedly vast in scale, the big twins retain a human dimension and quality. Components are easily changed, which means a rider can effect improvements to the bike's looks or performance Because of this an owner builds a relationship with his mount, whereas slickly-finished imported bikes merely challenge riders with their stratospheric abilities. In this way, Harleys appeal to riders who really want their motorcycling to be an emotional experience, or to create an image. The vast distances of the USA are still best conquered by large-capacity, low-revving power units, regardless of the fact that the V-twin is no longer the most efficient space/power unit. So the current range comprises three closely-related variants of this engine configuration.

The XLH Sportster is motorcycling stripped to its bare essentials. There aren't that many parts, and what there are are out on show in the breeze. Americans like it because the Sporty has been on the scene in one shape or form since 1957. The current 54 cu in/883 cc (76 × 97mm) engine is of unit construction unlike its bigger brothers, and has the time-honoured peanut gas tank perched above the cylinders. On the premium price models there isn't

even a passenger seat or pegs, tachometer, and absolutely no frills or gadgets. Only recently have bikes been given a 5-speed transmission, and a belt drive to the rear wheel on the 883 cc de-luxe and 1200 cc versions. Harley make very little profit from the low-price, entry-level Sportster, apparently, but what they do get is new customers and new allegiances. Many graduate up the range and buy another, more expensive Harley

Three styles of big twins dominate the range, all sharing the massive 80 cu in/1340 cc Evolution motor. The "modern-looking" FXR range carries conventional suspension systems front and rear, and a variety of sport or custom themes wrapped around emotive names such as Low Rider and Super Glide. There's also a light-tourer, in the guise of the FXRT Sport Glide with handlebar fairing and panniers. The closely-related FXD bikes such as the now-deleted Sturgis and limited-edition Dyna Daytona feature the recently developed Dyna Glide chassis for that long, low look.

In contrast the Softails, designated FXS and FLS, are a range of bikes sharing a method of rear

Launched at Daytona, Florida in 1992, this magnificent "Nostalgia" version of the 1340 cc Heritage Softail is typical of Harley-Davidson's ability to see where they're going and where they've been. It combines 1950s retro looks with 1990s custom styling. The monochromatic treatment includes whitewall tyres by Dunlop and Fresian cow-like leather trim for the seat and saddlebags. After the Fat Bob and Fat Boy models, some wags were predicting that this elegant bike was about to be called the Fat Cow. Whichever name is adopted, it's a long way from the "Silent Grey Fellow" – the first V-twin bikes created 80 years earlier.

suspension reminiscent of the rigid hardtails produced by various customisers. The look is one of minimalistic non-suspension at the back, but there's actually a pair of gas-charged extending dampers ingeniously hidden under the transmission between frame tubes! Here the Heritage Classic conjures up memories of the early tourers, while the Springer employs a frontal suspension not seen on a Harley for decades. And the bulbous Fat Boy is a bike that only one manufacturer would dare to create, and its based in Milwaukee. The FLSTF encapsulates a look, and that look is fat.

There are any number of technologically advanced touring motorcycles available to the long-distance rider now, but only one has a pedigree that stretches back many decades – the Electra Glide. The legendary "King of the Highway" FLH has the mass to stand up to headwinds, sidewinds and everything that an 18-wheeler barrelling down the interstate can throw at it. The distinctive handlebar-mounted fairing remains for protection, while luggage is swallowed by a cavernous pair of panniers and king pack. Its tour-style companions, the Glide Sport and Tour Glide, also demonstrate it takes more to build a tourer than a computer, some fancy electronics and a fairing.

Conventional suspension fore and aft characterises the FXR range of Harleys. Back in 1972 the Super Glide appeared as a stripped alternative to the FLH, or perhaps a Sportster for those who preferred the bigger 74 cu in/1200 cc mill. Rakish front forks characterised the Low Rider – now in its 15th year of production and arguably the start of factory custom machines. The first FXRS was introduced in 1982, while radical belt-drive arrived in 1983. This one is the FXRS-Conv Low Rider Convertible, to give it the full handle. It comes as standard with Lexan windshield and ballistic nylon/leather saddlebags, both featuring quick-disconnect hardware so they can be removed in a matter of moments. Highway pegs suspended from the front downtubes provide a relaxed riding position. A sissy back seat is included for the pillion's comfort, and further hints towards the "laid back" character of the bike.

ABOVE *Cast aluminium 16 inch rear wheel in Softail rear end is major feature of FXSTC Custom, and contrasts nicely with the skinny, spoked 21 incher up front. Other features to note include buckhorn bars, highway pegs and standard sissy bar. That rear suspension may hark back to the chopper-style hardtails of the '50s, but its 4 inches of wheel travel sure make it easier on the kidneys.*

RIGHT *Harley-Davidson's Heritage Softail, first seen in 1985, and the Classic, launched in 1987, made the world sit up and take notice thanks to their blend of modern technology and nostalgia styling. The Classic added a windshield, studded seat and saddlebags, sissy bar and attractive two-tone paint on tank and fenders over and above the regular Heritage. New improved saddlebags came in for 1990; but above all else the bike, like all other Harleys is dominated by the engine, in this case the V2 1340 cc Evolution mill*

OVERLEAF *Harley-Davidson's budget-priced entry-level model – the 54 cu in/883 cc Sportster – has been a part of the American landscape since 1957. As with all Harley models, a series of improvements were introduced gradually over the years. 12 volt electrics appeared in 1965, and an electric start option two years later. 1969 saw battery ignition to replace the magneto, and '71 a wet clutch. Around this time, a Sportster-powered streamliner ridden by Cal Rayborn set an absolute speed record at the Bonneville Salt Flats, reaching 265.492mph – just a bit more than a proddie bike! In 1972 Harley-Davidson temporarily forgot their conservatism and wheeled out a beefy 61 cu in/997 cc machine – the XLCH 1000. This one pushed out 61bhp and could reach 116mph. The particular bike shown here has a special paint job, masses of extra chrome (much of it engraved), plus drag pipes. One to take to Sturgis, or Daytona, and turn knowledgeable heads.*

LEFT *FLT Tour Glide model was added to range in 1980 to supplement the Electra Glide. The major difference is in the fairing, which on this bike is larger and mounted rigidly to the frame. It was the first Harley to ever sport a 5-speed transmission. The two-tier seat gives great comfort for rider and passenger, the latter has grab rails if the former gets ragged. Due to a dry weight in excess of 700lb, top speed can't quite reach three figures. Then again, you'll probably appreciate that when the time comes for an emergency stop – it's always best to allow extra distance between you and the vehicle in front,* *unless you intend to imprint the shape of that lovely mudguard into someone's trunk. Many admire Harley's links with the past, but dearly wish the brakes were of a more modern and efficient bent. The FLT's forte is loafing along two-up with all the luggage you can carry, at a comfortable 50–60mph.*

ABOVE *The "plain" Heritage Softail appeals to the rider who seeks the essence of American motorcycling. But as braking power is limited to a single disc up front, it's also advisable to look where you're going...*

ABOVE *All Harleys have links with past models, but some shout it louder than others. The FXSTS Springer with its Forties-style front fork proudly proclaims its ties with the past. The efficiency of the "reborn" springer forks is greatly improved over the originals, thanks to the addition of a modern gas filled hydraulic damper suspension unit. Cleverly Harley-Davidson have blended this in so as not to distract from the 1940s style. The forks dominate the appearance so much that the tiny chrome halogen headlamp is reduced to the status of a pimple. But it sure puts the excitement back into night-time riding…*

LEFT *Elongated fishtail silencers, chrome tool box and whitewall tyre reinforce the custom message of this 1340 cc Evolution-powered Softail.*

UPS AND DOWNS

It's in the suspension department that the FXSTS Springer Softail, (left) launched in 1988, creates most interest. At the rear, it's pure '57 hardtail-lookalike nostalgia while at the front, the distinctive external springs create a lean appearance, echoing a system which was last fitted to a factory bike in the '40s. Lots of Harley cruisers feature feet-first highway pegs as standard, and those that don't soon seem to have them fitted. On this and other Custom Softails, the laid-back pilot soon learns to adapt himself to the machine, especially in the area of control operation. Gear-shifting requires a deliberate foot movement away from the rest position, so smart getaways tend to be accompanied by a series of jerks when viewed from the left side. Not as smooth as Cary Grant. FLSTF Fat Boy (below) wears Hydra Glide-type front forks carrying a 16 × 3-inch solid disc wheel in cast aluminium; and into the '90s, the retro look is in with a vengeance at the back – no visible means of support.

LEFT *Ultra versions of Electra Glide Classic and Tour Glide full dress bikes arrived in 1988 sporting various high spec gizmos such as cruise control and a CB intercom/radio. Leg guards were standard also. Owners of "bare" FLHs can add them from the accessory catalogue, as they fit easily onto the crashbars. They're available colour matched for the various factory paint schemes used over the years, or in primer only.*

ABOVE *The Japanese manufacturers have turned to retro bikes to bolster sales, but Harley-Davidson are the ancient guardians of that particular niche. The Sportster, if anything, is the ultimate example of the retro genre, as it's been in production so long that it's gone out of and come back into fashion. What hasn't changed is the big-V cadence which announces that internal combustion is spoken here in capital letters – there's no way you'll ever*

think you're riding an electric motor. That also means vibes reach the rider through the bars, pegs and saddle. Only if you spend a whole day perched on the seat will the vibes grate, but the chances of doing that are remote anyway. The stylishly small 2.3 gallon gas tank ensures you climb off every hundred miles or so, as those giant cylinders drink juice at the rate of around 50mpg. Gentle touring will see 60mpg, while stop-go urban riding using gears and brakes alot will drag the consumption down to the 40mpg mark. A dry weight well below 500lbs gives respectable rather than drag-strip performance, but an 883 will certainly keep up with bigger V-twins thanks to lower mass. A 14 second quarter-mile sprint being typical. As you are now travelling in excess of 90mph, it's time to think about stopping with plenty of anticipation of solid objects – the discs front and rear on modern Sportsters are acceptable but hardly powerful.

Belt rear drive, jointly developed by Harley-Davidson and the Gates Rubber Company of Denver, Colorado in the late '70s, has distinct advantages over other motorcycle drive systems. Whereas an exposed chain attracts dirt and debris like a magnet, a toothed belt is lighter, cleaner and quieter, requires no lubrication and far fewer adjustments. Shaft drive, though clean and relatively maintenance-free, adds weight and complication to a bike, robs it of power, and introduces handling quirks as the throttle is opened or closed. It has been calculated that the belt employed on Harleys is up to 98% efficient, which means more of the power produced by the engine is transmitted to the rear wheel. Life expectancy is also three times that of a conventional chain. A tensile cord of aramid fibre is the core of the belt, providing incredible strength and durability with great flexibility. Protection for the teeth is provided by a heavy nylon fabric and a special polyurethane. Though resistant to stretching, the belt flexes sufficiently to absorb the shocks occurring during power transmission or gear changes. The finish of the belt also reduces noise, as a rubber on metal contact is inevitably quieter than a metal on metal system. The only requirement asked of the rider is that tension is checked every 2500 miles, so no wind-up jokes. This of course invokes the question "so what's new?" The first Harley, in 1903, surprise, surprise from the retro kings, used belt drive too!

ABOVE *Tour Glide, introduced in 1980 to partner the Electra Glide, was the first Harley to sport a rubber-mounted motor. Triple discs are needed to stop the 1000lb-plus that the bike weighs when a rider and luggage are added. In an emergency stop, slowing down on a Harley used to give the rider the impression of one of those supertankers that takes miles to grind to a halt. But the FLT at launch had the largest braking area of any H-D ever. The first models employed an enclosed chain to drive the rear wheel, complete with oil bath. The housings flexed with the swinging arm and gave a life of up to 20,000 miles. Seating accommodation was via a proper dual seat, though a sprung version giving a higher seat height was also available. Other improvements to handling and agility were made by mounting the fork tubes behind the steering head. More ground clearance – 2 inches better than the contemporary FLH – meant greater angles of lean up to 35° from vertical were possible. While this wasn't 45° sportbike territory, it was better than any previous big Milwaukee tourer.* (David Goldman)

RIGHT *The Dyna Glide Daytona and Custom models, each with a glowing pearl finish, are the first to pass through Harley-Davidson's new £13 million paint plant at York, Pennsylvania- a 90,000 square foot building which puts the scale of the company's original premises in some perspective. Here the environment is controlled and scrupulously clean, and not a speck of dust or dirt is permitted to blemish the paintwork on a gas tank or mudguard. A cluster of robot-controlled sprayers work on components controlled by a bar code system – there's no danger of wrongly coloured parts being fitted to a bike, and the days of flies embedded in tanks are thankfully consigned to history. All this smacks of some kind of loss of tradition, but nothing could be further from the truth. Harley-Davidson never make changes for change's sake – only when there's a definite improvement to be had. Robot painters bring greater consistency and efficiency to paint application. Changes of colour take a few seconds, as opposed to hours, for example. But graphics and pin stripes will continue to be applied by the craftsman's hand.*

ABOVE *Like the big FL tourers, the lighter FXRT Sport Glide boasts a natty, solenoid-controlled anti-dive unit on the front suspension. This neat sport-tourer was launched in 1983 – basically an FXR with 30-odd pounds of ABS plastic touring accessories added. Low gearing giving some 2700rpm in top at 60mph produced good gas consumption, averaging in the high 40s. This gave the 4.2 gallon tank a range of around 180 miles before hitting reserve or refuelling. Accessories offered included a matching touring box, luggage rack/sissy bar (both fitted here), a set of four extra instrument gauges, and a couple of radio systems for the mid-size fairing. You can even add a pair of legshields for serious touring duty.*

RIGHT *Seats and carrying capacity of FL tourers are amongst the best in the business. The studded rider and passenger perches give real "armchair" comfort enabling hundreds of miles to be covered without stopping to recover the feel of limbs, while the panniers and King Pak swallow a surprising amount of stuff. This Ultra Classic Electra Glide also features rear speakers for the passenger's benefit. Is there a better place from which to view the States?*

RIGHT *Riding impressions of the Heritage are mixed. Sure, you cut a heroic profile, and when engine speed is up to that steady cruising lope, vibration isn't a problem. At all other times, you feel those tremors loosening your fillings. That's because the Heritage engine is bolted directly to the frame, not rubber-mounted like the Low Riders and FL tourers. All Softails have this feature, but opinion is divided as to its popularity – there are many who would trade some of those visceral vibes for a little more comfort. Rubber-mounted floorboards and handlebars at least help make the Heritage driveable, though the former touch down at the slightest provocation. The chrome half-dome front hub gives a wide-eyed view of your location, but permits just one disc up front – that means braking power is compromised, and the rear disc has to be brought into play often. Then again, do you really want to go that quick on this sickle? The Heritage is rock steady when sweeping through curves at reasonable speeds, but push harder and a gentle wallow reminds the rider that this is not a point-and-squirt sportbike. Driving lights either side of the headlamp improve night visibility.*

OVERLEAF *Studded saddlebags on retro-look FLSTC Heritage Softail Classic are well made and keep their shape, even when empty. This is down to the stiff, saddle leather construction. Three teardrop Harley logos find homes on each bag between all the studs and buckles. On the down side, they don't hold a great deal. Other nostalgic elements include twin 16 inch spoked wheels, fishtail silencers, tall Lexan windshield and chrome half-dome front hub. Though the bike evokes touring Harleys of decades earlier, this one functions efficiently, with rear suspension, disc brakes that can actually stop forward progress rapidly, and a reliable, oil-tight Evolution engine.*

ABOVE *Heralding a new blend of smoothness with style, the 1991 FXDB Sturgis employed a Dyna Glide chassis with simpler two-point isolation mountings to subdue vibrations from the all-black 1340 cc V-twin. Though its appearance closely resembled that of its ten year old namesake, the new Sturgis featured an oil tank located under the transmission, drive belt set outside the frame, and an anti-theft device. This sump-type oil system tidied up the outer appearance, and made assembly easier as the mill could be placed in the frame already plumbed in. An ultra-low seat height of just 26.6 inches – just below that of the 1991 Hugger Sportster – was possible because of the compact frame construction. An internal steel frame with a single backbone is employed. On the move, the Sturgis rider can feel the imbalance of the power pulses, but at no point do the vibes hinder the enjoyment of riding. Some of the big twins, such as the rubber-mounted FXRs, have become so bland at cruising speeds as to fall out of favour with many Harley enthusiasts.* (David Goldman)

RIGHT *Latest 1200 Sportster is much improved, with vastly rehashed engine, smooth-shifting, shorter-throw gear change and belt final drive. The traditional peanut tank remains, however, to ensure just short bursts of about 100 miles are possible between gas refills. By that time, you'll be wanting to get your butt off that seat anyway. The Hugger version of the 883 Sportster, introduced in 1979, has a lower, narrower perch to enable the shorter rider to fit comfortably on the machine and paddle it around at low speeds.* (David Goldman)

ABOVE *Electra Glide Sport, launched in '87, is the stripped version of the 1340 cc touring FLHT Electra Glide. Less weight means extra zip, but against this is the lack of certain creature comforts. A more basic specification means plain "police" screen and panniers unfettered by protective crashbars. This owner has added colour-matched leg guards and a King Pack to his machine.*

RIGHT *Anyone jumping onto an 883 cc Sportster in a European country after riding smaller-capacity Japanese bikes is in for something of a shock. The performance is poor because the engine is restricted – all European-spec bikes are produced to the toughest, Swiss regulations, which means the carb and exhaust strangle the horses. This gives the fabulous looking large V-twin all the stomp of a 250 cc Honda Super Dream. There are two courses of action open to Sportster owners – to either accept the bike as it is, or switch the offending bits for others which liberate more of the engine's potential. The only snag with the latter option is that any parts change makes the bike illegal, as it no longer conforms to Type*

Approval. Sadly that isn't the end of the story. Further hard currency would need to be lavished on better rear shocks and front stoppers, in addition to the bits already mentioned. Together these bits mount up to a four figure sum, which seems crazy when added to the high European price of the basic bike. While the Sportster may be fine toodling around the States at 55mph, at faster European cruising speeds the vibration soon becomes a trial of the riders' resolve.

OVERLEAF *The most expensive touring motorcycle a pile of dollars can buy is the Ultra version of the Electra Glide Classic or Tour Glide Classic, first launched in 1988. The FLHTC and FLTC still feel like gen-u-ine motorcycles, yet give all the creature comforts and conveniences that modern touring riders demand. Look out for the digital clock, sound system, CB intercom, cruise control and that essential accessory, the cigar lighter. That means the dry weight is a considerable 765lbs. Add 5 gallons of fuel, a couple of bikers and their luggage and the whole moving thing weighs almost half-a ton!*

ABOVE LEFT *As this 1977 74 cubic inch FLH 1200 Electra Glide illustrates, progress wasn't exactly hurried by the Harley-Davidson factory. With the factory in the doldrums over quality, jokes about the iron-barrel V-twins proliferated, usually revolving around its agricultural character. Some farmers out west even threatened to use the Harley to pump water! Having said that, there was much about the FLH that was right anyway – the riding position was spot on for long distances. This model sports the "King of the Road" package, comprising windshield with small leather bag mounted behind, spotlamps, fibreglass saddlebags with guards, mirrors and safety bars front and rear.*

LEFT *Those who have been privileged to see the legendary Electra Glide being assembled inside the factory come away with mixed opinions. To some the experience is almost mystical, while more sceptical types have likened it to watching a line of elephants being dressed up in Christmas tree lights!*

ABOVE *Combinations provide even more surface area for the Harley-Davidson fanatic to adorn with custom statements. The colour-matched beige and cream sidecar hitched to the inevitable Electra Glide is substantially built and even has a matching wheel. In poor weather a cover can be clipped onto the studs for extra protection against the elements. Perhaps "The Strong Survive" is an oblique reference to the handling.*

LEFT *Instrument cluster of modern Electra Glide is
functional but not very ornamental. Intercom controls
are on the tank just behind the giant chrome plated filler
cap. Although the specification now boasts a tacho and a
maze of warning lights, the old tank mounted speedo
was much admired, if not really practical.*

ABOVE *The paintwork on the Softail is as it left the
factory, instantly recognizable from Arkansas to Zurich.
But many riders, of course, want to stand out from the
crowd, and it's a desire Harley-Davidson not only
acknowledge, but encourage. With over 50 candy and
pearl colours – to be bought from your Harley-Davidson
dealer, naturally – and of course endless automotive
colours to choose from, every machine can make a
unique statement.*

CHAPTER FIVE

STYLE COUNCIL

In the country of their origin, obtaining entry to the cult that is Harley-Davidson comes relatively cheaply. A little over $4000 opens the door, in the shape of the basic 883 cc Sportster, though you can also spend double this on a big-bore model. What they don't tell you in the advertising blurb is that these "basic" bikes need a fair amount of money thrown at them to make them go and stop acceptably, and another large chunk of money to start fooling around with the looks – this treatment marks the bike out as a personal statement. Welcome to the world of customising and open your wallet wide, folks.

Quite clearly, Harley culture just begins with the purchase of the bike. Each and every bike becomes a rolling picture frame for a rider, a reflection of self image. This explains why H-D Inc now comprises three divisions – motorcycles, accessories and collectibles. The latter provides stylish Harley-Davidson things you can wear and fripperies and trinkets you can keep about your home. Naturally the logo is emblazoned large upon each item, just in case anyone's missed the message you're trying to ram home. This designer paraphernalia is clearly a part of the business the company treats very seriously, as it

no doubt makes handsome profits and serves to reinforce marque allegiance. I mean, who's going to collect all this stuff, and then go out and buy a Yamaha?

H-D Inc's Motor-Clothes division, launched in 1989, symbolises the expansion in aftermarket Harley products that mushroomed during the 1980s. This department, who incidentally sponsor the Harley Dirt Track racing series, has sufficient items in the range to fill a 40-page catalogue. The very latest venture in this area, announced in early 1992, is, believe it or not, designer swimsuits! Not something you'd immediately think of in connection with the primordial V-twins, but heck, there's a few bucks in it.

The simple reason why Harley-Davidson sought a (larger) piece of the action is because they couldn't miss the number of private outfits who supplied bits and pieces to customise owners' bikes. The harsh reality that bog-standard machines rolling off the production line just didn't perform or look right spawned an army of custom houses. By mail order or over the counter, these fed a market hungry for accessories – everything from humble washers up to complete, tuned motors. Better shocks and brake components also did a roaring trade, or you could

swap the whole frame if necessary.

Alongside the bits that made a Harley go, handle and stop respectably, Harley owners also sought to personalise the appearance of their mounts. Why own a bike that looks like everyone else's, when you can make it a unique statement on two wheels? Owners began to turn their mounts into monuments to chrome and fancy paint, depending upon the depth of their bank balances. Some even bedecked their Harleys with rubies and sapphires, which might be taking things just a bit too far.

Now, when attending any gathering of the marque, you can only marvel at the precocity and sheer variety of the schemes that Harley owners can invent. The age of the bike is immaterial, as the number of Panhead and Shovelhead customs easily match the later Evolution-powered machines. Take your sunglasses with you, as those acres of chrome and garish colours can be hard on the eyes otherwise.

ABOVE *Massive rear rubber (in this case a BF Goodrich) is sometimes for effect, and sometimes there for a purpose – it depends whether the drag bike is a replica or real. In stock trim the big V-twin engine only pushes out some 70bhp or so, and top speed is 55mph, officer. Try telling that to the quicker dragster pilots. In 1991 Bill Furr, Pro Star National Champion, blasted his Top Fuel Harley through the quarter-mile in a boggling 7.26 seconds, with a terminal speed of 188.35 mph. To achieve that sort of stomp, you need a massive print from the rear wheel.*

OVERLEAF *This bike started out as a 997 cc (81 × 97mm) '69 Ironhead Sportster, but has undergone radical surgery since. The hardtail frame and steeply raked forks emphasise the long, low, lean look, while the Comstar alloy wheels, disc brakes, leading axle forks and wild paint scheme further distance the bike from its modest XLH origins.*

ABOVE *To watch a craftsman apply pinstripes to a tank or mudguard by hand is quite a nerve-wracking experience – for the observer, that is. These guys often do their business in bike shops or at gatherings surrounded by lots of ogling punters. But you won't see a tremor or a quiver sully the paint – remarkable. The "5" on the Sportster tank decals denotes a five-speed 'box.*

RIGHT *Not content with the regular perch, the owner of this Electra Glide has replaced it with a sumptuous, padded diamond seat for the ultimate in comfort. An extra backrest for the driver provides support and reduces fatigue.*

OPPOSITE *Studded leather saddlebags on this elderly Harley Hydra-Glide echo the notion of the bike as the iron horse. Having those white fringes so close to the hot exhaust pipe doesn't look so clever, though.*

LEFT *"She's an Eagle when she flies", screams the Eagle tank artwork; if this isn't enough the engraved air cleaner box will reinforce the message on this superb FLH 1200 Electra Glide which has been shorn of its fairing*

ABOVE *Arlen Ness is regarded by many as one of the most imaginative customisers of Harley-Davidsons. This incredible creation, typical of his bold approach, drew a constant stream of admirers. Note the one-piece headlamp fairing and tank unit and the streamlined rigid rear treatment. All Harleys turn heads, but this is one machine guaranteed to make you stand out in a crowd.*

RIGHT *Stylish Fat Bob tank comprises two linked chambers, each with its own gas cap and fuel tap. To fill the tanks to the brim, you have to fill up one side, then the other. Why? because only one cap is vented. Usually the join between the halves is covered to hide the frame member. Note also pizza-size, alarm clock style speedo, calibrated in kilometres only.*

WHY THE LONG FACE?

About 60 miles down the road from Daytona in Florida is Disneyworld. Here, grown men and women parade round in costumes pretending to be oversize mice and other furry animals. But Main Street during Bike Week is crazier by a long chalk. Harley-Davidson offer more accessories than any other marque: chrome fork tube covers, baloney-slice muffler pipes, gas tank panels, coil covers, "Buckhorn Pullback" handlebars, the list is daunting. Add to this the leathers, the boots, the "future Harley rider on board" maternity top – yes, that's what I said – the watches, the beach towels, the removable tattoos, and you'd think anyone would be satisfied with the *official* H-D gear. As these pictures show, there's just no pleasing some people. You won't find this one in the official Harley catalogue.

ABOVE *If balancing the gyroscopic effects of two wheels is a bit of a problem, why not have three – trikes are an accepted part of the custom scene. This Shovelhead has been effectively recycled into a practical and stylish cruiser. Note the neat two-into-one exhaust system and how the bobbed rear fender has been retained above the new axle. The number plate is good, but who chose the paint colour? The first Harley trikes were the factory produced Servicars of the 1940s and 1950s.*

ABOVE RIGHT *The stump-pulling torque of the Sportster is legendary, and can rocket a bike away from a standing start. But a handful of power-crazed folk hanker after even more grunt, like from two engines mounted side by*

side. Just look at the size of those forks, that petrol tank, and the rear fender. Asbestos trousers look a good idea too, judging by the proximity of those exhaust pipes to the right leg. No doubt it's brilliant in a straight line, but I wouldn't like to see it take a hairpin bend.

RIGHT *It never rains in California, so they say, and it looks as if the owner of this glorious hardtail custom steed never sees a drop when he's riding, either. Otherwise those fancy upturned silencers would act as unintended water butts. Don't you just love the flames on that deeply valanced fender – even the chrome stays holding it in place are curved.*

104

ABOVE LEFT *Attend a large gathering of Harleys and you must prepare yourself for all manner of custom treatments. This immaculate Heritage Royale, based on a Softail, carries overtones of Bugatti pre-war styling according to its creator. Note the see-through front fender enveloping the forks, headlamp nacelle, air cleaner, extra body sections and peek-a-boo rear wheel. Way over the top or the epitome of good taste?*

LEFT *Very few Harleys hide their beautiful, sculptural engines behind all-enveloping fairings, but this machine is built purely for one purpose – speed. Lurking underneath all that fibreglass streamlining is a highly tuned 1340 cc Evolution motor. This has been specially tuned by Carl's Speed Shop of Santa Fe Spring, California. Note slick rear tyre, 3-spoke alloy front and solid disc rear wheels.*

TOP *Cruising around the States demands an open face helmet, and naturally you can get one with your favourite bike endorsed on it.*

ABOVE *Someone has made the ultimate HOG statement on his bobbed rear fender. Though believe it or not, this is an official Harley accessory.*

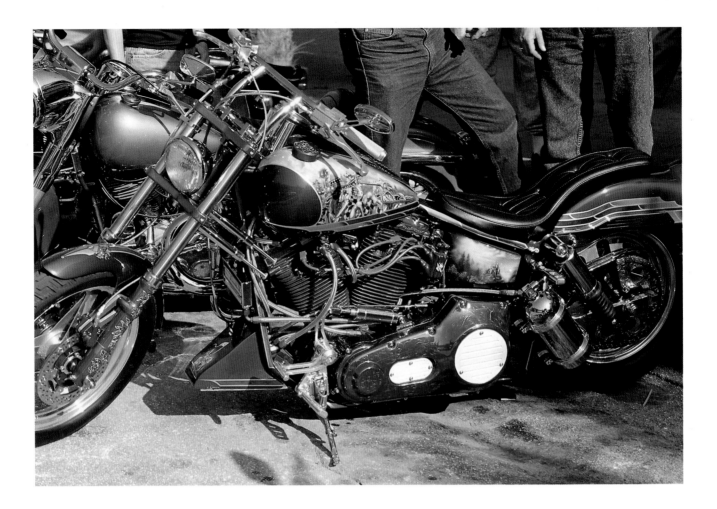

ABOVE *Co-ordinated purples and turquoises form the backdrop for jousting knights and hill-top castles on this amazing 1340 Low Rider. Fine engraving on the front fork legs, petrol caps, chaincase cover and rear sprocket give onlookers plenty to admire.*

RIGHT *This 1340 cc V2 Evolution v-twin engined device is a mixture of different models produced to meet its owners individual requirements. The dummy kickstart adds to the period feel which its creator has set out to achieve; tank mounted instrumentation also helps.*

LEFT AND ABOVE *Red cylinder barrels and purple cylinder heads to match the rest of the bike's paintwork – almost anything goes when it comes to Harley customising. The days when a frame was rubbed down to bare metal, primed and then glossed are long gone, as the whole process of painting has become much more refined and scientific. Powder coating has become the technique to use, as it is more chip, crack and peel resistant than conventional liquid paints. Nor does it fade or corrode, so the durable finish keeps its freshness and sparkle for years. Painted engine parts like those on this bike are possible with polyester versions of powder coating – these dissipate heat more efficiently to allow the engine to run cooler.*

RIGHT *Little danger of anyone running into this FLH Electra Glide after dark.*

LEFT *The key to a top quality result like this is twofold – preparation and powder coating. Here are the steps to take. First clean all parts thoroughly by blasting them with a jet of silicon glass beads. Frames are usually sand blasted. Then place the parts in a jet spray washer – an industrial machine not unlike a dishwasher – to remove all grease and debris. Further cleaning and etching in a series of tanks then takes place, to scrupulously clean the surfaces and prepare them for maximum powder adhesion. Only at this stage are parts dried, masked up and hung for powder coating. Powder particles are given a positive charge and therefore cling to the negatively charged parts. Once the powder has been applied, the parts are cured in an oven and then allowed to cool. Accent colours or details can then be applied, before the final crystal gloss powder gives a clear coat to increase its depth and provide a maintenance-free surface.*

It's even possible to apply a clear coat of powder to aluminium parts too. Tests have shown that a part submerged in sea water for a year still didn't tarnish, so road conditions are a breeze in comparison. Just think of it, no more polishing. Take your choice from matt and glossy finishes, and opaque, candy or glitter "colours" according to taste, and wait for the bill. At least now you know why it costs so much!

ABOVE *There's an exception to every rule, and here's the one that disproves all modern-day Harley riders are fashion freaks. This real tourer with home-made leg guards was spotted rolling up to a summer gathering of American V-twins at Baildon, Yorkshire, England; August 1990. Basis of the machine is a disc braked FLH 1200.*

ABOVE *If you want to get yourself noticed 1) buy a Springer Softail; 2) wear a gold lame outfit with matching helmet and boots; 3) be a female rider. If you want to get yourself REALLY noticed, comply with all three above criteria.*

OPPOSITE *Utah sunset – the rock formations and wide open spaces of the prairies make a fitting subject for custom paint on this 1340 FLHTC Electra Glide Classic tourer.*

RIGHT *Yeah, a Springer Softail guarantees it, man.*

LEFT *For many the sheer starkness of the standard XLH Sportster is a major plus, as there are less parts to strip off so that customising can commence. There are parts and accessories available to make the Sportster into just about any type of motorcycle you wish. There are literally mountains of bolt-on bits to alter the style, comfort or power characteristics of the bike. Owners of older chain-driven models can add a belt-drive rear transmission. This Sportster motor carries painted air cleaner and points covers. Note also folding highway pegs.*

TOP *Contemporary steeds like this Softail from the Harley stable pack rather more than just one horsepower, but conjure up for their owners similar notions of freedom as a four-legged friend. Broad areas of custom paint enable individuals to reveal just what's on their minds – this owner has made that connection with the Wild West about as clear as it can be.*

ABOVE *Fancy a different kind of Sportster, for just $75? Then cruise over to your local Harley dealer and put your best foot forward. This model has a full grain leather perforated body upper, with a solid rubber wing outsole. So now you know. Other models include the Heritage and the Sneaker.*

ABOVE *Here's one accessory you won't find in the official H-D catalogue. Just the thing for when some mad car driver tries to share your piece of tarmac...is it a Colt 45?*

ABOVE RIGHT *If you're riding a Harley, you know you're riding a Harley. You don't need to look in the mirror to remind yourself which marque you're aboard, but this reminder is pretty neat. these days the vibes are sufficiently damped down to permit a shake-free rear view image to be seen too.*

RIGHT *Home-spun customising is commonplace. Here a couple of HOG gas caps accompany some zany striping and a couple of eerie faces peering from the speedo. Weird.*

ABOVE *Neatly created Sportster custom mimics XR750 dirt racer with high-level pipes and Kerker silencers. Note the huge twin-calliper, floating disc brake on the front wheel though – the real thing just had a skinny hub and you stopped when engine braking dictated the thing stopped rolling! Other technical details of this superb bike include Italian Forcello (read Ceriani) front forks, oil cooler, alloy rims and rear set footrests.*

CHAPTER SIX

GATHERINGS

Where do you hang out if you want to grab an eyeful, and an earful, of HOGs? In Britain, make a beeline for Style Street, alias King's Road – the trendy bit of Chelsea that suddenly becomes a small slice of America on any sunny summer afternoon. There are so many booming Glides, Sportsters and Customs thronging the place that you'll turn more heads by droning through on a Jap race replica. Whether you'll generate the same level of envy among the onlookers is another matter....

America, favoured by a more hospitable climate in many states, has Harley gatherings, big and small throughout the calendar. Many are unofficial meetings based around eateries or Harley dealerships, while the two largest organised events of the year occur in Daytona Beach in Florida and Sturgis, South Dakota.

Bike Week in Daytona at the beginning of March marks the start of the riding season for many motorcyclists – who can blame them? There's the ocean on three sides, warm weather, bars aplenty and ladies wandering around in skimpy bikinis. Oh and there's bikes, thousands of them, mainly Harleys of course. Then there's the auctions, rodeo, swap-

meet, raffles to win Harleys, road racing, supercross, dirt track racing, an enduro, drag racing... and Main Street. Sometimes it seems that 99% of the people attending Daytona – estimates vary from 150,000 to 500,000 depending on the source – are all trying to cram into the main drag at the same time. Certainly a quarter of a million doesn't seem impossible when you've been part of the crush.

The other main Harley event is Sturgis in early August. This spot by the Black Hills in South Dakota is, for 50 or so weeks a year, home to a paltry 7000 innocent inhabitants. In early August, however, many of the locals flee, as hordes of bikers descend upon the town. Some estimates put the 1991 attendance at 500,000, though the actual figure is probably well below this.

Bikers began flocking to Sturgis a half-century ago, to attend a short-track race meeting. Half-mile dirt track races are still held there during the modern rallies, and everybody who sees them comes away just knowing they've seen some gen-u-ine, no holds barred competition. Elsewhere, countless thousands of bikers are cramming themselves into fields, setting up tents, opening the odd can of

refreshment and in general living life to the full.

Once towards the end of the 1970s, H-D's vice-president of styling and famous grandson – Willie G Davidson – turned up at Sturgis on an experimental belt-drive Lowrider. Harley buyers generally like their bikes to strongly echo the past, but this daring technological advance was greeted with plenty of enthusiasm rather than a lynching. What might be regarded as a most positive piece of market research resulted in the belt-drive progressing towards full production. Other aspects of the bikes' styling and mechanics are often discussed by Harley executives and everyday riders at meetings like these.

Wherever Harleys gather, at meetings small or large, you're guaranteed a warm welcome. Take the people for what they are – bike enthusiasts, not troublemakers – and you won't go far wrong.

ABOVE *Main Street is the place to be during Bike Week at Daytona, especially as daylight gives way to darkness. The atmosphere created by all those Harleys and happy people just has to be experienced. Spirits are high but trouble is rare, especially as the police are a constant presence.*

OVERLEAF *When you tire of Main Street, the beach is a good place to blow away the cobwebs. Daytona Beach first gained a reputation for racing in the early part of the 20th Century, and no less than thirteen auto racing records were set on the beach up to 1935. Motorcycle racing officially began on the long strip of sand in 1937, and continued to 1961, with a break for the World War II between 1941-47. Racing moved to the current site at the International Speedway in 1961. Maximum speed on the beach is now a leisurely 10 mph. The beach is 23 miles long, 18 of which are accessible to traffic, and up to 150 metres wide. The slope of the hard-packed sand to the water is very gentle – almost flat. Many visitors cruise up and down on beach buggies, quads or special bicycles with wide tires. The Sportster shown is a 997 cc XLCH dating back to the early 1970s.*

ABOVE *Never one to miss an anniversary, Harley-Davidson celebrated 50 years of rallying at Sturgis, South Dakota with this limited edition 82 cu in machine. Introduced in 1980 the FXB Sturgis ran 106 mph maximum speed on 65 bhp. Factory records show 1470 were built in the first 12 months of production.*

OPPOSITE *It's advisable to get down to Dresser shows early, if you want a clear view of all those pristine FLs. Try taking a shot from late morning until dusk, and you can guarantee that someone from the throng will step in front of your lens.*

RIGHT *Wherever a bunch of Harleys assemble, you'll find ZZ Top impersonators thick on the ground. Even the factories they make the bikes in are full of the Lone Star state group's lookalikes.*

Racing transferred to the International Speedway at Daytona in 1961 because competition on the beach had become too dangerous. The winner of the first Daytona 200 was presented with the trophy in 1937. By 1951 prize money worth $2500 was added, while the 1991 winner, Miguel Duhamel, took home more than $40,000 in prize money and awards. A racing museum still resides back at the original site – visit the Birthplace of Speed Museum at 160 Granada Boulevard in Ormond Beach. A stone's throw from Daytona International Speedway is the Municipal Stadium, home of the dirt track racing during Bike Week. The 10,000 seat stadium has a banked quarter-mile track, and events take place under floodlights. Action shows 1991 883 Sportster.

Nancy Delgardo hustles her 883 cc Sportster around the Daytona International circuit. Harley-Davidson Twin Sports racing is the hot class at the moment, as it provides close competition on a minimum budget. The series has run since 1989 in the USA, and there's a new eight-meeting series in the UK in 1992. Most of the British Harley dealers will be campaigning, together with some magazines and loads of privateers. Even if you can't see the action all that well, you'll hear it – the roar made by hordes of lusty V-twins is marvellous.

LEFT *Smiles and good humour abound at any Harley gathering, as this night view of "Main Street" proves.*

BELOW *There was a time when motorcyclists preferred their steeds and their riding clobber in honest to goodness black. But not anymore. Now bright and breezy poster colours are very much in, especially yellow. It certainly brightens up the scene and gives motorcycling a far better image to Joe Public.*

OVERLEAF *The boys come out to play at night.*

LEFT AND OPPOSITE *No age limit – you don't have to be a young gun to pose around town on the Harley. Maybe it's the white beards, but many of the guys trickling along Main Street at Daytona look like they should be pottering around the garden or enjoying a leisurely round of golf. But who gives a damn?*

ABOVE *Helmets are now compulsory in most US states, but here's one design you won't find in the glossy brochures. It's also adorned with stickers which indicate the owners' delicate sensibilities.*

RIGHT *A Harley rider tests the seams of an XXL T-shirt.*

BELOW *Main Street at Daytona Beach, and the bikes and bikers are on parade. So that's what they mean by a chain reaction.*

OVERLEAF *Customised Springer Softail driven to Cheltenham, England by West German H.O.G. member.*

LEFT *Early March in Florida '92 – a recipe for some Springtime sunshine, surely. Yep, except for one day, when freak conditions towards the end of Bike Week at Daytona saw some of the worst weather in the region for forty years. A typhoon, hailstones of substantial size and an afternoon of torrential rain didn't stop the bikes rolling, though. This guy didn't even bother to put anything over his T-shirt! Says a lot for the protection offered by the 1340 cc Electra Glide Ultra's fairing and leg shields.*

ABOVE *Start 'em young and bikes will be in the blood for a lifetime. Not just any old make, of course.*

*Policemen, Hells Angels, accountants, poseurs – there's
no telling what a Harley dude does for a living.*